PRIMARY SOURCES TEACHING KIT

World War II

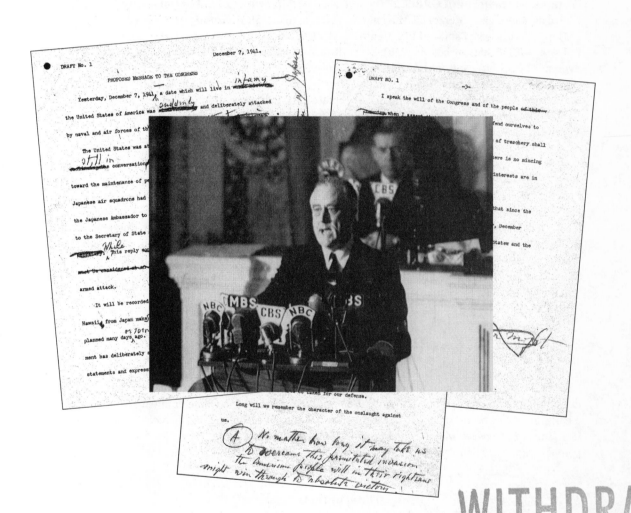

by Sean Price

New York • Toronto • London • Auckland • Sydney
Mexico City • New Delhi • Hong Kong • Buenos Aires

Teaching *Resources*

To the memory of my father, David Price, a soldier in the war

Edited by Linda Scher
Picture Research by Dwayne Howard
Cover design by Norma Ortiz
Interior design and illustration by Melinda Belter
Map design by Jim McMahon
ISBN: 0-439-51896-2

2 3 4 5 6 7 8 9 10   40   09   08   07   06   05   04

Contents

INTRODUCTION

Using Primary Sources in the Classroom

Seen as a point on a world history time line, World War II happened just yesterday. Yet to today's students, World War II may seem like an ancient epic. Fortunately, World War II was amply documented. New media such as movies and radio became increasingly critical to communicating ideas during this period and supplemented letters, diaries, photographs, and other more established forms of communication in documenting the war. This wealth of firsthand sources allows students to see an "old" war from many new angles.

Primary sources offer a wealth of other benefits for your students as well. Textbooks often present a single interpretation of events; primary sources compel the reader to supply his or her own interpretation. A thoughtful analysis of primary sources requires both basic and advanced critical-thinking skills: determining point of view, evaluating bias, classification, comparing and contrasting, and reading for detail.

Primary sources can also help students recognize that the artifacts of our contemporary lives—a ticket stub, a school report card, a yearbook—may one day be fodder for future historians.

One of the most important steps in teaching history is to help students understand the difference between primary and secondary sources. Share the chart below to demonstrate the categories to your class.

MATERIAL	DEFINITION	EXAMPLES
Primary Sources	Documents created during or immediately following the event they describe, by people who had firsthand knowledge of the event	Letters, diaries, photographs, artifacts, newspaper articles, paintings
Secondary Sources	Documents created by people who were not present at the event that occurred	History books, biographies, newspaper articles

Keep a folder handy with copies of the primary source evaluation form on page 19. Encourage students to complete this reproducible as they study each document in this book. Eventually, this kind of analysis will be automatic for your students as they encounter primary sources in their future studies.

Using the Internet to Find Primary Sources

The Internet can be an amazing tool for finding primary sources. Just remind your students to take extra care to verify that the source is reliable. Here are a few outstanding sites for using primary sources in the classroom:

Library of Congress: **http://www.loc.gov**

National Archives Records Administration: **http://www.nara.gov**

http://www.spartacus.schoolnet.co.uk/2WW.htm Online encyclopedia provides an excellent overview of the war accompanied by relevant firsthand accounts.

http://www.fordham.edu/halsall/mod/modsbook45.html#Lead Up to War Fordham University site contains many firsthand documents about the war

Ask your students to find other great sites for primary sources and create their own list. Keep a running list, posted near a computer terminal.

Background on World War II (1939–1945)

World War II was the most destructive human event in history. Its impact can be compared to natural disasters like the Black Death of the 1300s. There's no accurate death toll. Estimates usually range from 30 million to 55 million. Some go as high as 100 million. But it's hard to know where to stop counting. For instance, do you include the millions who died in the years after from wounds or trauma?

Likewise, the war had many causes. They include economic and political instability, Adolf Hitler and Nazism, Japanese imperialism, the Treaty of Versailles, European anti-Semitism, Allied appeasement, the Great Depression, and American isolationism, among others.

It is vital for today's students to understand World War II because this conflict touches us still. The world's current system of treaties and alliances sprang from the war. America's colleges and public school systems were shaped by the baby boom that followed the war. Our interstate highways are modeled after the autobahn that Germany used during the war. In a sense, we are all children of World War II. The primary sources in this book will help explain why.

About This Book

Studying World War II can be daunting. The first Nuremberg war-crimes trial alone produced 42 volumes of testimony. Yet those volumes focused almost exclusively on the conduct of Nazi leaders—a few people fighting for one side of the war. World War II's overall record includes millions of photos, movies, newsreels, radio transcripts, reports, posters, diaries, memoirs, artifacts, and official papers. This book provides a small sampling of these documents.

World War II also presents students with many complexities. Consider the question, Who fought on what side? There is no simple answer because several countries shifted allegiances. For example, the Soviet Union began by helping Germany to carve up Poland. Later, the Soviets themselves became Nazi victims. The terse diary of eleven-year-old Tanya Savicheva reprinted here records the destruction of her entire family during the nearly 900-day siege of Leningrad by the Germans.

The documents included in this volume reveal other complexities of the war as well, such as the attitudes of average soldiers. On one hand, American servicemen, like their fellow citizens, were united in their goal of defeating the Axis powers. That is one reason World War II is often remembered as the "Good War." But the "Willie and Joe" cartoons by Bill Mauldin show that American GIs actually fought two wars: one against the enemy and the other against U.S. Army regulations.

The final section of this book provides statistics about the war's cost, both in lives and dollars. These figures help put in a larger context the firsthand sources that chronicle the war's personal side—the memoir of a thirteen-year-old girl at the gates of Auschwitz, the final letter of a Japanese kamikaze pilot, and a Marine airman's letter pondering his bizarre new life in combat. These and other documents show today's students the true cost—and the true legacy—of World War II.

World War II Time Line

NOVEMBER 1923 Adolf Hitler, leader of the fledgling Nazi Party, leads a failed attempt to overthrow Germany's weak democracy, called the Beer Hall Putsch. He is sentenced to five years in jail for treason but serves only nine months. While in prison, Hitler begins writing *Mein Kampf.*

OCTOBER 1929 The U.S. stock market crashes, plunging the world into the Great Depression. This weakens democratic political parties in Germany and Japan.

SEPTEMBER 1931 Japan seizes Manchuria. This begins an on-again, off-again war with China that eventually leads to the Pacific conflict with the Allied forces. Throughout the 1930s, militarists gradually weaken Japan's civilian government, leaving the army and navy in control.

JANUARY 30, 1933 Adolf Hitler is appointed chancellor of Germany. He soon consolidates power and becomes dictator. The German government passes laws depriving Jews of their citizenship, forbidding them to use public facilities, and excluding them from almost all professional jobs.

MARCH 7, 1936 German troops enter the Rhineland, a part of Germany where they are forbidden to go by World War I's peace treaty. France and Great Britain do nothing.

MARCH 12, 1937 German troops peacefully take over Austria. Great Britain and France do nothing.

SEPTEMBER 30, 1938 Following a policy of appeasement, Great Britain and France agree to allow Germany to take over a huge area of Czechoslovakia called the Sudetanland. British Prime Minister Neville Chamberlain says of the agreement, "I believe it is peace for our time."

MAY 1939 Germany and Italy form a military alliance called the "Pact of Steel." Japan joins the alliance in 1940 to become the third Axis power.

AUGUST 1939 Scientist Albert Einstein sends a letter to U.S. President Franklin Roosevelt recommending a research project to create an atomic bomb. It prompts the creation of the Manhattan Project.

AUGUST 1939 Nazi Germany and the communist Soviet Union, previously sworn enemies, sign a nonaggression pact. They secretly agree to invade Poland and other nearby countries and divide all territory taken.

SEPTEMBER 1, 1939 Germany invades Poland. Britain and France soon declare war on Germany. World War II begins.

MAY 1940 Germany attacks Western Europe, overrunning Holland, Belgium, Luxembourg, and France in about six weeks. Chamberlain resigns as British prime minister and Winston Churchill takes over. Italy joins the war on Germany's side.

JUNE 22, 1940 France surrenders to Germany.

JULY 10, 1940 The Battle of Britain begins and continues until May 1941.

1941–EARLY 1943 German submarines sink more than 2,000 Allied ships while suffering few losses. By May 1943, Allied antisubmarine tactics and weapons turn the tide against Germany in the Battle of the Atlantic.

FEBRUARY 1941 Germany sends troops to North Africa to help Italy conquer this area. Battles rage there until 1943, when Germany and Italy are finally forced out.

JUNE 22, 1941 Breaking the nonaggression pact, Germany launches a surprise invasion of the Soviet Union.

DECEMBER 7, 1941 The United States enters World War II after Japan launches a surprise attack on the U.S. Pacific Fleet at Pearl Harbor, Hawaii. Japan also launches widespread attacks across the Pacific, building a huge empire in six months.

JANUARY 1942 At the Wannsee Conference near Berlin, top Nazi officials finalize details for the "Final Solution," their plan to kill all of Europe's Jews.

JUNE 4, 1942 At the Battle of Midway, U.S. planes sink four Japanese aircraft carriers. This battle is a turning point in the Pacific War. Japan never goes on the offensive again.

AUGUST 7, 1942 Marines land on the Japanese-held island of Guadalcanal. It is the first attack in the U.S. "island-hopping" campaign to Japan.

JANUARY 1943 The United States and Britain step up bombing of German cities and military targets, creating a round-the-clock assault.

JANUARY 31, 1943 Soviets defeat Germans in the Battle of Stalingrad, blunting Hitler's invasion of the Soviet Union and ending his successful conquests.

JULY 9, 1943 Allies invade Sicily. Within two months, Mussolini is forced from power and Italy surrenders. However, German troops occupy much of Italy and fighting continues there.

JUNE 6, 1944 (D-DAY) U.S.-led Allies land at Normandy in France and begin the campaign to liberate occupied Europe.

JANUARY 27, 1945 Auschwitz death camp, in operation since spring 1940, is liberated by Soviet troops.

APRIL 12, 1945 President Franklin Roosevelt dies of natural causes. Harry Truman becomes president.

APRIL 30, 1945 Hitler commits suicide as Russian troops close in on his underground bunker.

MAY 7, 1945 Germany surrenders unconditionally. The next day is VE-Day (Victory in Europe).

AUGUST 6, 1945 The United States drops an atomic bomb on Hiroshima, Japan. On August 9, the United States drops a second bomb on Nagasaki.

AUGUST 14, 1945 Japan surrenders unconditionally. The following day is VJ-Day (Victory over Japan).

TEACHING NOTES

Prelude to War

Use with page 20.

BACKGROUND

Adolf Hitler was a frustrated painter who dreamed of becoming an artist; he was a decorated soldier in World War I and, later, a brilliant public speaker and strong leader. Hitler was also one of the most monstrous dictators of the twentieth century.

Hitler first tried to seize power in 1923 in Munich in the "Beer Hall Putsch" (revolt). It failed, but Hitler turned his treason trial into a forum for his racist, anti-democratic ideas. A sympathetic judge sentenced Hitler to the minimum of five years in a comfortable prison (he served only nine months). During this time he began writing Mein Kampf, *or* My Struggle.

At the time, the Nazi Party, officially called the National Socialist German Workers' Party, had few members. Though Hitler was not taken seriously by the party leaders, he refused to become discouraged. When the Great Depression destabilized Germany's already weak democracy, Hitler used the situation to his advantage. In 1933, Germany's conservative politicians and military leaders supported him for chancellor, believing that he would be a pliable pawn. Hitler quickly consolidated his power and never looked back.

Mein Kampf *helped to rally faithful Nazis and get out Hitler's message. At first sales were puny, but by 1933 only the Bible outsold it in Germany. Young couples often got a copy as a wedding gift, and virtually every home had it displayed. Nevertheless, comparatively few people actually read the whole book—nearly 700 pages filled with Hitler's repetitive, rambling prose.*

But those who read even part of Mein Kampf *got a preview of Nazi Germany. As William L. Shirer put it in* The Rise and Fall of the Third Reich, *"For whatever other accusations can be made against Adolf Hitler, no one can accuse him of not putting down in writing exactly the kind of Germany he intended to make if he ever came to power and the kind of world he meant to create by armed German conquest."*

TEACHING SUGGESTIONS

⊠ Ask students what they know about Adolf Hitler. Then have them read the quotes. What is their tone? What can your students tell about this man?

⊠ Discuss the problems that post–World War I Germany faced (loss of territory, hyperinflation, war reparations, weak government) and ask how a politician like Hitler might capitalize on those problems. How does he make use of these issues in the quotations? What does the photograph of Hitler show about the image he might want to project as a leader?

⊠ Have students read the quote on using terror in politics. Then have them research the three main organs of terror in Nazi Germany: the SA, SS, and Gestapo. What were these organizations? How did they live up to Hitler's statement in *Mein Kampf?*

⊠ Explain that the League of Nations was the forerunner to the United Nations. Then have your students reread the final two quotes. What are Hitler's plans? Why might other people ignore such warnings?

Hitler Youth

Use with page 21.

BACKGROUND

Adolf Hitler understood the importance of indoctrinating children at an early age. The Nazis skillfully channeled their energies for political purposes. Their main tools were public schools and the Hitler Youth. Teachers were expected to instill in their pupils Nazi social values and teach Nazi racial theories, at the cost of the traditional curriculum.

Hitler also tapped in to one of the strongest youth movements in the world. About 10 million young people belonged to youth groups that were usually tied to churches and other institutions. By 1936, all of these groups had been absorbed into the Nazi youth movement. In 1939, membership became mandatory. Parents who objected faced prison sentences or had their children taken away.

The Hitler Youth was the best known of five Nazi youth groups. Boys belonged to the Jungvolk *(Young Folk) from ages 10 to 13, and the Hitler Youth from 14 to 18. Girls belonged to the League of Young Girls from ages 10 to 13, the League of German Girls from 14 to 17, and Faith and Beauty from 17 to 21. Aside from indoctrination, these organizations stressed physical fitness. Boys trained to become strong soldiers; girls were expected one day to bear lots of children.*

Not all German youths accepted the Nazis' rigid discipline and conformity. Lower-class teenagers often formed criminal gangs that warred with the Hitler Youth. And "Swing Kids" were upper- and middle-class teens who grew long hair, dressed in unusual clothes, and listened to swing music, which was banned for its African-American roots. Nevertheless, few German boys or girls escaped the Nazi influence. One German opponent of Hitler wrote, "Their supremacy over the German child, as he learns and eats, marches, grows up, breathes, is complete."

TEACHING SUGGESTIONS

- ☒ Use Evaluate That Document! (page 19) to consider these artifacts and documents. Taken together, what do they say about Hitler and the Nazi Party? About being a good German citizen?

- ☒ Many historians have argued that the Nazi Party was as much a religious cult as it was a political movement. What elements of these artifacts and documents have religious overtones? How might they have made young people more committed to Hitler's cause?

- ☒ Have students read the Hitler Youth oath and the U.S. Pledge of Allegiance. Explain that both were meant to be recited while standing before a flag. Compare and contrast the two oaths. You might have students paraphrase the two pledges to grasp their meanings better. (For a history of the U.S. Pledge of Allegiance and its original phrasing, see National Flag Day's **http://www.flagday.org/Pages/PledgeHistory.html**.)

Hits of the 1940s

Use with page 22.

BACKGROUND

World War II produced many famous songs. Some were amusing, like "Der Fuehrer's Face." Written by Disney composer Oliver Wallace, it was originally used as part of a Donald Duck cartoon by the same name. Humorous songwriter Spike Jones turned the song into a hit that played frequently on the radio.

"Der Fuehrer's Face" was meant in part to make fun of the Nazi habit of opening and closing almost every human transaction with "Heil Hitler!" Erika Mann, a German who opposed Hitler, wrote in her book School for Barbarians:

"Every child says 'Heil Hitler!' from 50 to 150 times a day, immeasurably more often than the old neutral greetings. The formula is required by law; if you meet a friend on the way to school, you say it; study periods are opened and closed with 'Heil Hitler!', 'Heil Hitler' says the postman, the street-car conductor, the girl who sells you notebooks at the stationery story; and if your parents' first words when you come home to lunch are not 'Heil Hitler!' they have been guilty of a punishable offense, and can be denounced."

Actress Marlene Dietrich, another German opponent of Hitler, became irrevocably tied to the war's number one hit song, "Lili Marlene." Dietrich was already internationally famous in 1935 when she left Germany for the United States. During the war she performed for Allied troops and spoke out against the Nazis. But it wasn't until 1943 that Dietrich first sang "Lili Marlene," a tune with an unusual history. It was written in 1915 by a German soldier in World War I. In 1941, a revised version abruptly became a hit among German troops. Allied soldiers hearing it on German radio fell in love with "Lili Marlene" even though most couldn't understand the lyrics. An English-language version was quickly written, and Dietrich turned it into her signature tune. No other song rivaled "Lili Marlene's" popularity on both sides of the European war. Sad and beautiful, it became an unofficial anthem for foot soldiers.

TEACHING SUGGESTIONS

- ☒ Familiarize students with foreign words or unusual terms in "Der Fuehrer's Face." *Fuehrer* is the German word for leader and refers here to Hitler; *Herr* is the German word for mister; Goebbels (pronounce GEHR-buhls) was Hitler's propaganda minister; and Goering (pronounced GEHR-ing) was the Nazi air force commander, second in command to Hitler. "Phhht!" is a raspberry or Bronx cheer.

- ☒ Use Evaluate That Document! to study the lyrics of both songs. What do the lyrics say? Why might songs like these be popular in wartime? What appeal does each song have?

- ☒ Play recordings of other popular World War II–era songs, such as "In the Mood" and "We'll Meet Again." Again, ask what message these songs might convey to an American audience and why they might be popular in wartime.

- Have each student do a brief report on a Hollywood star who contributed to the U.S. war effort. Students should be able explain why that star was famous and what contribution he or she made. They should also explain wartime terms such as "war bonds" and "USO."
- Have students research the Civil War song "Lorena." Like "Lili Marlene," it became the number one hit on both sides of a war. How is it similar to "Lili Marlene"?

Propaganda

Use with page 23.

BACKGROUND

Propaganda is a one-sided form of communication meant to shape opinions. Some scholars include all kinds of advertising or educational materials in that definition. Others say the word applies only to those emotional appeals that mislead or distort. Hitler's brilliant propaganda minister Joseph Goebbels relied heavily on propaganda to mislead the public. "Any lie, frequently repeated, will gradually gain acceptance," he said.

The Nazis did not invent the use of propaganda. In fact, the word propaganda *took on a negative meaning after World War I, when the public learned that all sides told lies as part of their effort to win support. However, the Nazis were masters at using propaganda, and they were among the first to systematically employ all media—film, art, speeches, writing, radio, and print channels—to get their message across. This naturally included posters, which offered a cheap and reliable way to reach a mass audience.*

Propaganda posters permeated life in nearly every Axis and Allied country. During World War II, posters could be found not only on military bases and in government offices but also in businesses, schools, and even homes. Some of them, like the Russian poster shown here, were blunt and visceral. Others, like Norman Rockwell's "Freedom from Fear" poster, were more subtle. All of them appealed to viewers' patriotism as a way to support their side's war effort.

TEACHING SUGGESTIONS

- Use Evaluate That Document! (page 19) to compare these three posters. Have students sum up in three words the appeal each poster has for its audience. For instance, the "Freedom From Fear" poster evokes parents' fear that their children

will not be safe. Among the many words students might use to describe its appeal are "home," "security," or "love."

- The "Freedom From Fear" poster is one of four Norman Rockwell posters based on Franklin Roosevelt's "Four Freedoms"—freedom of speech, freedom of worship, freedom from want, freedom from fear. Have students research the Four Freedoms. Why were they important? How does Rockwell's series portray Americans enjoying their freedoms? What wartime messages might an audience read in them?

- Have students vote on which poster they feel is most effective and which they feel is least effective. Tally the results and use them to lead a discussion. Did one poster lead the voting in either category? Ask your students why they voted as they did. Have the results changed their opinions? In what ways are the posters like modern ads in magazines or on billboards?

- In wartime, it is common for one side's propaganda to portray the other side as less than human. This is seen in the Russian poster comparing Nazis to bugs. Have your students find other examples of posters (from World War II and other wars) that use this propaganda technique. Have them discuss the type of animal or insect used. Why was it chosen? What feelings does it arouse?

Radio Days

Use with page 24.

BACKGROUND

Radio broadcasting was less than two decades old when World War II began in 1939, but it had already become the best and fastest way to convey information. Radio played a prominent role in keeping British spirits high during the Battle of Britain, Hitler's first major defeat.

After Germany's stunningly rapid conquest of France in 1940, Great Britain stood all alone against Germany. The United States had not yet entered the war. The country's new prime minister, Winston Churchill, commanded a demoralized army that had lost most of its tanks and heavy equipment at Dunkirk. But Hitler had problems as well. To get an army safely across the English Channel, he needed control of the skies. Almost everyone assumed the German

air force, the Luftwaffe, would make short work of Britain's Royal Air Force (RAF), but that didn't happen. Though badly outnumbered, RAF pilots had two big advantages: the Spitfire fighter plane and a secret weapon called radar. The Luftwaffe got mauled, losing about two airplanes to every one for the British. The RAF's determined defense led Hitler to postpone his invasion.

For almost a year, as the air war raged, Churchill used radio to keep British hopes alive with some of the greatest do-or-die speeches in history. The Germans replied with English-speaking broadcasters like William Joyce (a British turncoat dubbed "Lord Haw-Haw" by listeners in England), who tried to undermine British morale. The still-neutral Americans were riveted by broadcasts from CBS correspondent Edward R. Murrow, who gave them a front-row seat to the plight of Londoners during the Nazi "blitz."

TEACHING SUGGESTIONS

✉ Acquaint students with Great Britain's retreat from Dunkirk, when British and Allied troops were forced to flee France for Britain. They had to leave many troops and much of their equipment behind to be captured by the invading Germans. Then have students use the Evaluate That Document! form (page 19) to study each radio broadcast. What are the differences and similarities between the excerpts? Remind your students that at the time of these broadcasts, radio was as important as television is today.

✉ Have a student read aloud the section from Churchill's speech. What words and phrases do they think make this a powerful speech? In what ways does Churchill accurately predict the future?

✉ Ask students what William Joyce (Lord Haw-Haw) is trying to accomplish with his speech. Given all the problems that the British had faced, is such a tactic effective? Could this approach backfire? Students should be able to explain their answers.

✉ Before Pearl Harbor, the U.S. public was strongly isolationist. Murrow's London broadcasts were credited with helping to change public opinion and increase U.S. support for the Allies. Ask students to consider what Americans might find appealing about this broadcast. How does Murrow put his listeners at the scene with him?

Movies at War

Use with page 25.

BACKGROUND

The movie industry was in its infancy during World War I, so movies played a relatively small role in shaping public opinion during that conflict. But the 1930s and 1940s were the golden age of motion pictures. During World War II, both documentaries and feature films became important weapons in the struggle for world opinion.

The most famous documentary of the period is the pro-Nazi Triumph of the Will directed by Leni Riefenstahl. Its subject is the Nazis' Nuremberg Party Congress of 1934. The film presents a spectacle of marching, speeches, and adoring shots of Hitler—deliberately manufactured for Riefenstahl's cameras in a way that may seem repetitive for today's viewers. It shows the great skill of Nazi leaders in staging mass meetings and manipulating their audiences.

In many ways, the 1942 film classic Casablanca is no less a piece of propaganda than Triumph of the Will. The Office of War Information, the U.S. propaganda office, enthusiastically endorsed its anti-Nazi message. Casablanca tells the story of Rick Blaine, the mysterious owner of Rick's Café Americaine in pro-Nazi, Vichy-controlled Morocco. Rick is a metaphor for prewar America, cynically refusing to get involved in disputes between the European refugees who have flocked to Casablanca and the Vichy police (along with their German overlords). Like America, Rick finally has a change of heart. In fact, the story is supposed to take place on December 2–4, 1941—right before Pearl Harbor.

Both movies won prestigious awards. For Casablanca, these included the 1943 Academy Awards for best picture, best screenplay, and best director. Not surprisingly, though, the movies' fortunes have been quite different. Today, Triumph of the Will is considered a work of dark genius and is interesting mostly to historians. Casablanca remains a film classic, one of the most popular love stories of all time.

TEACHING SUGGESTIONS

✉ Use Evaluate That Document! to compare the still and photos from these two movies. Ask students to consider the differences in how the two movies portray Nazis. What words would students use to describe the appearance of Nazis in *Triumph of the Will*? (How does Riefenstahl select her shots of soldiers?) What words would they use to describe Major Strasser in the *Casablanca* still?

☒ View the first scene from *Triumph of the Will* where Hitler arrives out of the sky. Nazi propaganda often cast Hitler in a religious light, referring to him with words and images such as "savior" of the German people. How might the scene reinforce that view? How does the oath on the dagger artifact on page 21 convey that message?

☒ View *Casablanca* or one scene from it. Perhaps the most overtly patriotic scene shows Rick's patrons in a singing duel with Nazi officers. Remind students that this movie was released in early 1943, when the war was still hanging in the balance. Why might this scene have appealed to American moviegoers of the time?

Air War

Use with page 26.

BACKGROUND

World War II was the first war in which aircraft played a decisive role. Some of the most vivid images of the war involve planes: Hitler's Stuka dive-bombers screaming out of the clouds, German and British fighters "mixing it up" in the Battle of Britain, Japanese Zeros strafing ships in Pearl Harbor, and swarms of Allied bombers pounding Germany and Japan.

Infantrymen looked down on pilots for their supposed soft living. After all, pilots had the luxury of resting safely at their bases after each mission, while ground troops had to slug it out nonstop. In reality, airmen simply faced a different set of terrors. The strategic bombardment of Germany alone cost the United States about 29,000 of its airmen killed and 44,000 wounded. That is more than the entire Marine Corps death toll of about 20,000.

U.S. airmen enjoyed personalizing their aircraft with nose art. Nose art, like the decorated "Waddy's Wagon" shown here, was often humorous. Other paintings had patriotic themes and still others touted racy pin-up images. In fact, nose artists produced so many pictures of scantily clad women that the Air Force finally censored designs and then stopped allowing nose art all together, bringing a unique form of folk art to an end.

TEACHING SUGGESTIONS

☒ Use Evaluate That Document! (page 19) to analyze this photograph. What does it say about life for bomber crews? Why might an individual touch like painting nose art be important for airmen in war?

☒ Waddy's Wagon was a B-29 Superfortress serving in the Pacific. Its eleven-member crew had the following jobs: pilot, copilot, flight engineer, bombardier, navigator, radio operator, top gunner, left waist gunner, right waist gunner, radar observer, and tail gunner. See if your students can tell from their positions in the painting which person did which job.

900 Days in Leningrad

Use with pages 27–28.

BACKGROUND

Many cities suffered during World War II, but the people of Leningrad suffered more than most. The Soviet Union's second-largest city was besieged by German armies from September 8, 1941, to January 27, 1944. During that nearly 900-day period, between 600,000 and 1.1 million people died of shelling, bombing, disease, and hunger—especially hunger. During the first months, Soviet troops were unable to get more than a trickle of supplies through German lines to the people inside the city. Existing on short rations, about 2.5 million residents shivered in unheated buildings as they ate dogs, cats, rats, glue, and worse in order to survive. Some turned to cannibalism. But as the diary entry from poet Vera Inber shows, people found more than one way to prey on each other.

Had the Nazis captured Leningrad, the city might have faced an even more terrible fate. "The Fuehrer has decided to have [Leningrad] wiped off the face of the earth," went a September 29, 1941, order from Hitler to his generals. "The further existence of this large city is of no interest once Soviet Russia is overthrown." Eleven-year-old Tanya Savicheva kept a kind of diary of the siege in one of her ABC books. After the letter of their first name, she listed each family member who died and the date of his or her death. Tanya herself was finally evacuated from Leningrad but died in 1943 of chronic dysentery.

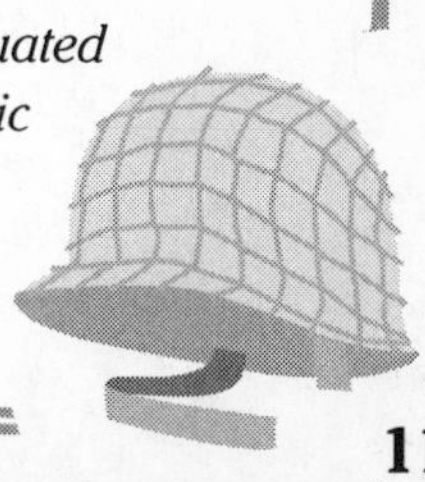

TEACHING SUGGESTIONS

✉ Use Evaluate That Document! (page 19) for each passage. Though one diary is written by an adult and the other by a young girl, both make powerful statements. You may want to explain the term "Lady Bountiful" to your students. Is the writer's use of it sincere or sarcastic?

✉ Compare and contrast the two documents. Ask students what they can learn about the siege from each. How does each convey the desperation felt by people trapped in Leningrad?

✉ During the worst of the siege, in the winter of 1941–42, laborers got a daily ration of no more than 1,087 calories. Office workers got less—about 581 calories, while children received about 684 calories. Have students find out how many calories a healthy person should have every day. How many does an average American get? What problems develop for people who do not get enough to eat over a long period of time?

✉ Have students evaluate the photograph of the winter scene. What does it reveal about the situation facing the people pictured? How does the poster in the center shape the scene? At whom might the warning be aimed? Why?

The Gates of Auschwitz

Use with pages 29–30.

BACKGROUND

The word "Holocaust" refers to the deaths of at least 6 million Jews under the Nazi regime. About 5 million non-Jewish civilians also died because of Nazi persecution. These included Roma (also known as Gypsies), Jehovah's Witnesses, homosexuals, and political prisoners.

These "enemies" of the Third Reich primarily died in a network of camps and ghettos centered around Germany and Poland. There were labor camps, transit camps, concentration camps, and extermination (or death) camps. The distinctions among camps reflected a difference in means, not ends. Labor camps and concentration camps tended to use inmates as slave labor, working them to death slowly. A strong inmate generally survived three to six months. The SS—the elite Nazi military force responsible for carrying out all aspects of Hitler's Final Solution, including the administration of the camps—called this

"annihilation through labor."

There were six death camps—all located in Poland: Auschwitz-Birkenau, Belzec, Chelmno, Maidanek, Sobibor, and Treblinka. All were designed specifically to kill Jews quickly. Only two combined concentration-extermination camps existed: Maidanek and Auschwitz-Birkenau (usually just called Auschwitz). As each trainload of victims arrived, SS doctors separated the weak, who died quickly in the gas chambers (disguised as showers), from the strong. The strong died slowly through labor, starvation, exposure, disease, or the whim of sadistic guards. SS Corporal Pery Broad worked at Auschwitz in the Gestapo, or secret police. Captured by the British shortly after the war, he wrote a lengthy description of Auschwitz's day-to-day workings. Broad's account ignored his own wrongdoing and was obviously meant to curry favor with the Allies. He served four years in prison after it was proved that he had helped with the selections.

Elli L. Friedmann was born in Czechoslovakia. She was living in Hungary in March 1944 when the German army invaded. Within two months, the Nazis had deported 437,000 people to Auschwitz. Only about 20,000 of them survived, including Friedmann. In all, about 500,000 of the estimated 750,000 Jews in Hungary died. Friedmann, just thirteen at the time, survived the war, while dozens of her friends and family perished. In her 1997 memoir, I Have Lived a Thousand Years: Growing Up in the Holocaust, *Friedmann (now known as Livia Bitton-Jackson) describes the selection process.*

TEACHING SUGGESTIONS

✉ Have your students use Evaluate That Document! for both memoirs. Both describe the same daily event—the initial selection process at Auschwitz. Ask what details these documents share. What differences do your students see between the person who observed the process and the one who went through it?

✉ The SS and their network of camps where thousands died daily were tools of a totalitarian regime. Ask students what laws and safeguards democracies such as the United States have in place to prevent the rise of a totalitarian government. In the twentieth century, genocide has taken place in Armenia, Cambodia, and Rwanda as well. Have students pick one of these and learn more about its causes.

Day of Infamy

Use with pages 31–32.

BACKGROUND

On Sunday, December 7, 1941, Franklin Roosevelt was eating lunch with his aide Harry Hopkins around 1:40 P.M. when he got word that Japan had attacked the U.S. Pacific Fleet at Pearl Harbor. At first neither he nor Hopkins could believe the news. Conventional wisdom had it that any Japanese attack would likely take place in the Philippines or somewhere else in Asia.

As the day wore on, it became clear that the United States had suffered a tremendous loss. Eight battleships, three light cruisers, three destroyers, and four other vessels had been sunk or badly damaged. At least 167 planes had been destroyed and another 128 damaged—most on the ground. More than 3,600 Americans were dead or wounded.

The grim afternoon that followed became a whirlwind of meetings, phone calls, and executive orders. Through it all, witnesses said, Roosevelt remained calm and steady. Toward evening he began dictating to a secretary the first draft of the message he would give Congress the next day.

Some cabinet members argued strongly that Roosevelt should make a long speech outlining America's relations with Japan. But Hopkins said the president "stuck to his guns, determined to make his statement to Congress what is in effect an understatement and nothing too explosive."

Roosevelt revised the speech right up to the time he gave it on December 8. As the draft shows, its most famous line—"a date which will live in infamy"—was one result of this diligent editing. The speech lasted seven minutes. Thirty-three minutes after it was over, Congress passed a resolution declaring a state of war between the United States and Japan. Within hours, Roosevelt had signed it. By December 11, Germany had declared war on the United States as well. Americans were now full participants in World War II.

TEACHING SUGGESTIONS

- Have students use Evaluate That Document! (page 19) to study the rough draft of Roosevelt's December 8 speech. How does it compare to the final version delivered to Congress? Did Roosevelt's editing make the speech simpler and more eloquent? Are there any changes that students disagree with?

- Ask students what word Roosevelt used repeatedly to describe Japan's intentions. Why might he have used it? What other words did Roosevelt use to emphasize Japan's treachery?

- Have students think about what is *not* in the speech. For instance, there are no estimates of U.S. dead or wounded, nor are there estimates of ships sunk or planes destroyed. Why might Roosevelt choose to leave this kind of information out or be vague in alluding to it?

- As Roosevelt states, he was Commander in Chief of the armed forces. However, under the U.S. Constitution, only Congress has the power to declare war. Why do students think the authors of the Constitution gave Congress that power? Why not give it to the president? Also ask students why they think Roosevelt waited until the last paragraph of his speech to ask for a declaration.

- Have students find out why many Americans adopted an isolationist attitude before Pearl Harbor. What historical events made them wary of foreign wars? Which lawmakers championed the cause of isolationism? Who argued against it? How did Pearl Harbor change those attitudes?

Soldier Life

Use with pages 33–34.

BACKGROUND

Few writers, photographers, or other artists captured the frustrations and hazards of GI life better than cartoonist Bill Mauldin. He joined the army in 1940 and took part in the invasions of Sicily and mainland Italy, earning a Purple Heart after being wounded. Trained as an artist, Mauldin began by drawing cartoons for his division's newspaper, and by 1944 he was a full-time cartoonist for the armed forces newspaper Stars and Stripes.

In 1944, Mauldin's book Up Front—a funny and moving essay about the war illustrated by his cartoons—remained number one on the best-seller list for 18 weeks. He also won the 1945 Pulitzer Prize for editorial cartooning (a feat he repeated in 1959). Mauldin wrote in Up Front, ". . . [N]obody who has seen this war can be cute about it while it's going on. The only way I can try to be a little funny is to make something out of the humorous situations which come up even when you don't think life could be any more miserable."

Mauldin's cartoons featured two perfectly average soldiers, Willie and Joe. Willie was supposed to be in his early 30s, while Joe was in his early 20s. Other than that, they were almost indistinguishable, except that Willie had a big nose and Joe had a little one. Together, they poked fun at common GI problems such as officers, food, weather, Army regulations, and just plain being afraid.

One aspect of life soldiers looked forward to was receiving and sending mail. As Mauldin put it, "A soldier's life revolves around his mail." Most letters written by soldiers were of the "Hi, how are ya?" variety—short and not terribly memorable as literature. However, some, including the long letter by Marine Lt. William Ellison to his friend, reveal great depth of thought.

TEACHING SUGGESTIONS

☒ Use Evaluate That Document! (page 19) to study these cartoons and the letter passage from *Up Front*. What is Mauldin's view of soldiering? Is it romantic? Is it practical? How does it compare with other images that students have seen in commercials and movies?

☒ Ask students about Mauldin's imagery in the passage from *Up Front*. Make sure they understand how the dangers he mentions correspond to those on a battlefield. For instance, the rattlesnakes are roughly equivalent to land mines and booby traps. The friend firing periodically represents sniper fire. The bull represents a tank. How might this passage be an effective way to give Americans on the home front a better understanding of a soldier's daily life?

☒ One of Mauldin's favorite targets was the petty tyrannies that foot soldiers endured. In the second cartoon, a smartly dressed officer is asking Willie why his uniform does not meet military regulations. Why might soldiers find Willie's reply amusing? Why might officers allow a cartoon that pokes fun at them to be printed in an armed forces newspaper like *Stars and Stripes*?

☒ Mauldin's cartoon showing German prisoners of war was daring for its time. It is one of very few Allied images to show German soldiers in a sympathetic light. Ask students how they can tell the one American soldier apart from the German prisoners. In what ways are they alike? Note the caption. Does the American soldier appear "fresh" or "spirited"? What point is this cartoon trying to make? Remind students that the audience was U.S. servicemen during the war.

☒ U.S. servicemen who fought in World War II (and those who made sacrifices or volunteered on the home front) have been called the "Greatest Generation." But as the last paragraph of Ellison's letter reminds us, most Americans did not see them that way at the time. In fact, newspapers and magazines were filled with stories about the frivolousness and immorality of young people. What might account for the change in the way Americans today view the soldiers of the 1940s?

☒ Have students paraphrase Ellison's distinction between physical and mental courage and discuss why he calls physical courage an "overrated virtue." Do students agree that adaptability is important during wartime?

Home Front I: Sacrifices

Use with pages 35–36.

BACKGROUND

In many ways, World War II was a boon for the U.S. economy. The demands of war production helped to finally pull the country out of the Great Depression and create full employment. Unlike Europeans, Americans at home did not have to worry about dodging shells or bombs. Physically untouched by war, U.S. factories and businesses became more prosperous as the war dragged on.

Americans did, however, endure hardships. One of the biggest inconveniences was rationing. About 20 items—including rubber, gasoline, liquor, and canned foods—were rationed because the resources used to produce or transport these goods, such as tin used for canned goods, were needed to produce or transport equipment and supplies for the troops. The first item rationed was sugar, in April 1942. The issuing of War Ration Book One to all Americans the following month created shortages of many other goods. It also led to a thriving black market in both rationed goods and phony ration books.

War Ration Book Two, shown on the poster in this section, was issued in February 1943. It limited purchases of certain goods by assigning these goods points and allowing each person a certain number of points per year. This system helped make the Office of

Price Administration one of the least popular federal agencies in U.S. history. However, the OPA prevented acute shortages and high inflation.

Anyone who grumbled about rationing likely heard the common reply, "Don't you know there's a war on?" This could be an insensitive thing to say to those whose loved ones were fighting overseas. Each day those families faced the nightmare of possibly receiving a Western Union telegram, such as the one shown here, informing them that a son, husband, or father had been killed or wounded overseas.

If the telegram announced that a soldier had been wounded, the family might not hear for weeks whether the injury had been fatal. Sometimes families of dead servicemen received letters from them postmarked after the date of their death. This raised hopes that a mistake had been made—that their loved one was still alive. Usually, it simply reflected the difficulties of sending letters from combat zones.

TEACHING SUGGESTIONS

⊠ Use Evaluate That Document! (page 19) to study these firsthand sources. Rationing was probably the aspect of the war that affected people on the home front most directly on a daily basis. Make a list of rationed items. Ask students to imagine how being without these items for weeks or months would affect them.

⊠ How do students think shopping with a ration book might be different from the type of shopping they do today? Ask them to notice directives on this government poster. How are people advised to alter their shopping habits?

⊠ Though they disliked rationing, many people found that it had beneficial side effects. The rationing of gasoline and rubber, for instance, caused traffic deaths to drop sharply. Can your students think of other ways rationing might have indirectly benefited Americans?

⊠ Have students consider the statement, "For a soldier's family, worse than receiving no mail was the appearance of the Western Union messenger at the door." What is the tone of the document? How does the clipped format contribute to this? You might explain that telegrams were the fastest, most dependable way to send messages during the war, but they demanded an economy of words.

Home Front II: Japanese-American Internment

Use with page 37.

BACKGROUND

Japanese Americans, who had faced decades of anti-immigrant prejudice, felt the repercussions of Japan's attack on Pearl Harbor sharply. Newspapers and lawmakers besieged President Franklin Roosevelt with requests to evacuate Japanese Americans from California, Oregon, and Washington state, reasoning that Japanese Americans would become spies and saboteurs if Japan invaded the United States.

On February 19, 1942, Roosevelt signed Executive Order 9066 authorizing the removal of anyone of Japanese ancestry from the West Coast. Approximately 110,000 people—70,000 of them U.S. citizens—were sent to ten internment camps. Stripped of their rights, these people either had to leave behind most of their possessions or sell them below market value. All of the internment camps were located in remote parts of the country, such as Heart Mountain, Wyoming, and Hunt, Idaho. Internees soon found themselves behind barbed wire in desolate surroundings, forced to live in communal barracks under the eyes of guards. Life at the camps was crude. Food and sanitation were poor. Everyday items like clothes had to be ordered through catalogs. All of the internees endured a lack of privacy.

Twenty-nine-year-old Miné (pronounced mee-NEH) Okubo was already an accomplished artist when she was forced to leave her home near San Francisco, travel to an "assembly center" in San Bruno, California, and then to the Topaz Relocation Center in the windy, barren Utah desert. Toward the war's end, Okubo became one of about 55,000 Japanese Americans who were allowed once again to live outside the camps. Before leaving Topaz in January 1944, she made a series of documentary sketches of camp life, which became the basis for her 1946 book Citizen 13660 *(13660 is the number the government designated for her last name). It was the first personal account of life in the internment camps ever published. Okubo became a successful artist after the war. She died in 2001.*

TEACHING SUGGESTIONS

⊠ Have students study the period just after Pearl Harbor. Ask them what the atmosphere was like in the United States. What types of comments and insults did Japanese Americans face? Why were anti-Japanese feelings so strong?

⊠ Use Evaluate That Document! (page 19) to study Okubo's cartoons. They show what life was like at the assembly center in San Bruno, California, where she spent about half a year. The camp was a converted racetrack, and her first "room" was a former horse stall. Ask students what kinds of life changes and issues the internees may have faced.

⊠ Japanese Americans lost an estimated $500 million because of the evacuations. In 1988, the U.S. government formally apologized and offered $20,000 to each person interned. Five years before, Okubo had written: "I am not bitter. I hope that things can be learned from this tragic episode, for I believe it could happen again." Hold a class discussion. What do your students think of the government's apology and offer of restitution? Do they agree with Okubo that such deportations could happen again?

⊠ About 26,000 Japanese Americans served in the U.S. armed forces during the war, despite the internment of friends and family. Several thousand served in the 442nd Regimental Combat Team and in the 100th Infantry Battalion. These units became famous for their bravery. Have students research their story and report to the class about what they find.

Women at War

Use with pages 38–39.

BACKGROUND

Women did everything that men did in World War II —fought in the front lines, shot down enemy planes, served as guerrilla fighters, patched up the wounded, led nations at war, won medals, reported from battle zones, served on ships, worked in war industries, and on and on. More often than not, women did all of this while men continued to doubt their abilities.

As a rule, countries that had been attacked directly—like the Soviet Union—readily used women in combat. Female snipers in the Soviet Red Army were especially deadly (one had 309 confirmed kills), and a group of their women fighter pilots were called "Night Witches" by the German pilots who feared them. On the other hand, countries that were more remote from the fighting—like the United States and Canada—tended to channel women into non-combat roles. A highly vocal minority in the United States opposed any role for women in the armed forces, but about 350,000 American women joined the military.

Around 75,000 women served in the traditional role of nurses. Other women served in specially formed units whose guiding slogan was "Free a man to fight." For example, the Women's Air Service Pilots (WASP) ferried airplanes around the country and occasionally took them overseas. The Navy's Women Accepted for Volunteer Emergency Service (WAVES) and the Women's Army Corps (WAC) took on noncombat jobs such as mapmaking, radar monitoring, and clerical work.

Newspaper ads, like the ones for WAC shown here, combated social criticism that military service would cause women to lose their femininity. Even in the service, women experienced frequent harassment and ridicule from servicemen. Yet 565 women in the WAC alone received the bronze star for meritorious service overseas. The best indication of their success was that the army asked to make the WAC program permanent after the war.

The image of one female welder, "Rosie the Riveter," became a symbol for women's commitment to the war effort on the home front. Female workers were motivated by patriotism and financial concerns: So many young men had gone off to fight that numerous vacant positions needed to be filled in factories that produced important wartime equipment. And there were also new economic opportunities available. The Great Depression had just ended in 1940, and assembly-line jobs paid well. A waitress making $14 a week might suddenly be able to make nearly $40 a week at a factory or shipyard.

Women struggled at first to gain the acceptance of male coworkers. They also struggled to get equal pay. Despite U.S. laws forbidding the practice of paying unequal wages for the same work, the average male factory worker made $54.65 a week while the average woman made $31.21. More than 210,000 women were permanently disabled in factory accidents, and at least 37,000 died. These women are never counted in the official casualty lists of the war.

TEACHING SUGGESTIONS

⊠ Use Evaluate That Document! (page 19) to analyze each of these documents. What do the ad and the poster say about attitudes toward women in the 1940s?

⊠ Show students some modern military recruitment ads. How do they portray women? How is that portrayal different from the World War II ads and posters?

⊠ Women had been working in U.S. factories for more than a century when World War II broke out. Yet the entry of so many women into jobs traditionally held by men had an enormous impact on American society. Ask students what message the poster conveys by setting an image of a pioneer woman loading a rifle next to a contemporary woman welding.

⊠ Ask students what words the song uses to describe a woman who is going to work on a factory line. What reasons are given to make the case for her joining the workforce? What about the duration of her work? Is it presented as a temporary or long-term change? How might the message play with different audiences, such as a young woman old enough to join the workforce or a middle-aged man whose factory line the woman might join?

A Fight to the Death

Use with page 40.

BACKGROUND

By late 1944, the Japanese were desperate. The U.S. Navy was at Japan's doorstep. The country's war-making industries had been starved of resources and bombed to a standstill. The Japanese had lost many of their best pilots, and their once-superior planes were now outnumbered by American machines.

With no hope of surviving by conventional warfare, the Japanese began using "kamikazes," or human bombs. The word "kamikaze" means "divine wind" and refers to the hurricanes that wrecked a thirteenth-century fleet sent by Mongol emperor Kublai Khan to invade Japan.

"Their patriotism was derived from their deep-rooted belief that the entire nation, society, and even cosmos was unified by and into the single Emperor, and for that cause they were willing to die," wrote one kamikaze officer who survived the war.

Suicide bombers baffled Americans. As Bill Halsey, a top U.S. admiral, put it: "Americans, who fight to live, find it hard to realize that another people will fight to die." In fact, the Japanese had to turn away volunteers eager to give their lives for their emperor, who was worshipped as a god.

The kamikazes first appeared during the battle for the Philippines in October 1944. But they made their biggest mark during the battle for Okinawa from March to July 1945. Of the 1,900 kamikaze attacks during that time, about 15 percent scored a hit. About 25 Allied ships were sunk, 157 were damaged by hits, and 97 others were damaged by near misses. One of those kamikaze pilots was Akio Otsuka, whose last letter is reprinted here. Overall, kamikazes killed or wounded 15,000 Allied fighting men, making them the Imperial Japanese Navy's deadliest single weapon.

TEACHING SUGGESTIONS

⊠ Use Evaluate That Document! to examine these two documents. What do they say about the Japanese military's mind set? How did Japanese airmen view life differently from Americans? (You might compare the letter from Akio Otsuka with the that of airman Ellison on page 34.)

⊠ One U.S. sailor wrote in his diary shortly after a kamikaze attack: "This gives you an idea what kind of an enemy were are fighting. . . . You do not discourage the [Japanese], they never give up, you have to kill them. It is an honor to die for the Emperor. . . ." How might this view, which was common among Americans, have led to the dropping of atomic bombs?

Hiroshima

Use with page 41.

BACKGROUND

In the early morning hours of August 6, 1945, the B-29 bomber Enola Gay was flying toward Japan. Copilot Robert Lewis heard that the secret weapon on board was armed and ready to be dropped. Lewis later wrote, "I had a feeling the bomb had a life of its own now that had nothing to do with us."

The Enola Gay's primary target was the Japanese city of Hiroshima, home to about 290,00 civilians and 43,000 soldiers. The atomic bomb about to hit Hiroshima was created by the supersecret Manhattan Project, which brought together the greatest scientific minds of the day.

The first combat atomic bomb, called Little Boy, exploded at 8:16:02 A.M. with a force equal to 12,500 tons of TNT. The temperature at the site of the explosion reached about 5,400 degrees Fahrenheit in less than a second. Just after the flash came an enormous blast. As one Japanese study reported, "Within 2 kilometers of the atomic bomb's hypocenter [the area under its detonation] all life and property were shattered, burned, and buried under ashes."

Little Boy killed about 70,000 outright. An equal number died of wounds, radiation sickness, and other illnesses by the end of 1945. A second bomb, called Fat Man, dropped on Nagasaki on August 9, killed 40,000 outright and an equal number by the year's end. The high death toll sparked a vigorous debate over President Harry Truman's still-controversial decision to drop these bombs. However, atomic bombs played a role in Emperor Hirohito's decision to surrender. The artifacts and photo in this section attest to the atomic bomb's awesome power.

TEACHING SUGGESTIONS

⊠ Use Evaluate That Document! (page 19) to study these photographs. What do they say about the extent of the destruction at Hiroshima? Which photo do students find most revealing about the city's fate?

⊠ People still argue about the morality of using atomic bombs. On one hand, these weapons resulted in death and horrible injuries for civilians. On the other, Japan was an intractable Axis enemy that had bombed U.S. territory. Many argued that dropping the bomb would shorten the war and save thousands of American and Japanese lives and would be better than a full-scale invasion of Japan. Break students into teams and have them debate. Make sure that they study the atomic bomb's historic context. Why were atomic bombs used on Hiroshima and Nagasaki? What debate among U.S. officials took place beforehand? How destructive was conventional bombing of Japan? What were Americans' attitudes toward the Japanese at the time, and vice versa? You might review with students the documents on kamikaze pilots (page 40) and on internment camps (page 37).

Aftermath

Use with pages 42–43.

BACKGROUND

Winston Churchill called World War II "the Unnecessary War." Indeed, many questions about it nag at the world's conscience. What if the democracies had stopped Hitler when he tore up the Treaty of Versailles or stood up to Japan early in its conquest of China? What if more had been done to save the Jews?

The answer is almost surely that the war would have been prevented or its death toll minimized. This notion has strongly influenced Western politics ever since, especially during the Cold War. In the 1962 Cuban missile crisis, for example, President Kennedy was ready to risk nuclear war rather than appear to be appeasing the Soviet Union.

The threat of nuclear attack was itself a by-product of the war. And dangers of a smaller sort linger as well. World War II–era bombs, shells, land mines, and grenades are still discovered regularly in old battlefields or at sea. No reliable figures are kept, but thousands of people have been killed or wounded by these discarded weapons since the war's end.

Reliable statistics on most aspects of World War II can be hard to find. Death tolls and costs are totaled differently by different researchers. Only estimates are possible. Nevertheless, the statistics here provide a broad overview of the war. As a counterpoint, the quotes show how the war affected people personally.

TEACHING SUGGESTIONS

⊠ Use Evaluate That Document! to study the statistics, quotes, and photograph. Point out to students that almost all wartime statistics are estimates because of the huge numbers involved and the chaos of war.

⊠ Virtually all statistics for World War II are higher than those for World War I. What factors might have caused this sharp rise? Which statistics do your students find most surprising? Why?

⊠ The Soviet dictator Joseph Stalin once cynically said, "A single death is a tragedy, a million deaths a statistic." What do students think of this statement? Do the numbers "6 million Jewish dead" or "30 million total dead" register in their minds? Or are they just numbers? Is it easier to understand the plight of one person, like the child who wrote the poem from the concentration camp or the U.S. soldier Charles Feinstein?

Evaluate That Document!

Title or name of document _____

Date of document _____

Type of document:

❏ letter   ❏ patent

❏ diary/journal   ❏ poster

❏ newspaper article   ❏ advertisement

❏ photograph   ❏ drawing/painting

❏ map   ❏ cartoon

❏ telegram   ❏ other _____

Point of view:

Who created this document? _____

For whom was this document created? _____

_____

What was the purpose for creating this document? _____

_____

What might the person who created it have been trying to express? _____

_____

What are two things you can learn about the time period from this primary source?

_____

_____

What other questions do you have about this source?

_____

_____

_____

_____

_____

PRELUDE TO WAR

At first, Adolf Hitler's *Mein Kampf* was ignored. But by the time he came to power in 1933, only the Bible rivaled its sales in Germany.

Adolf Hitler and his air force chief, Herman Goering, greeting a crowd in Berlin on July 6, 1940. Germany had just conquered France.

Quotes from *Mein Kampf*

As a young man, Hitler learned what he believed to be the recipe for winning and holding political power.

> "I achieved an equal understanding of the importance of physical terror toward the individual and the masses. . . . Terror at the place of employment, in the factory, in the meeting hall, and on the occasion of mass demonstrations will always be successful unless opposed by equal terror."

Once in power, Hitler promised to regain lands that Germany had lost after World War I.

> "We must clearly recognize the fact that the recovery of the lost territories is not won through solemn appeals to the Lord or through pious hopes in a League of Nations, but only by force of arms."

He also vowed to find *lebensraum*, or living space, for Aryan Germans. He believed that Russia's vast stretches would provide the best—but not the only—source.

> "We National Socialists [Nazis] must hold unflinchingly to our aim in foreign policy, namely, to secure for the German people the land and soil to which they are entitled on this earth. . . . If we speak of soil in Europe today, we can primarily have in mind only Russia and her vassal border states."

Primary Sources Teaching Kit: World War II • Scholastic Teaching Resources

HITLER YOUTH

On being a member of the *Jungvolk:*

"Far from being forced to enter the ranks of the *Jungvolk,* I could barely contain my impatience and was, in fact, accepted before I was quite 10. It seemed like an exciting life, free from parental supervision, filled with 'duties' that seemed sheer pleasure. Precision marching was something one could endure for hiking, camping, war games in the field, and a constant emphasis on sports . . . . To a degree, our pre-war activities resembled those of the Boy Scouts, with much more emphasis on discipline and political indoctrination. There were the paraphernalia [pins, ceremonial daggers, and so on] and symbols, the pomp and mysticism, very close in feeling to religious rituals. One of the first significant demands was the so-called *Mutprobe:* 'test of courage,' which was usually administered after a six-month period of probation. The members of my *Schar,* a platoon-like unit of about 40–50 boys, were required to dive off the three-meter board—about 10 feet high—head first in the town's swimming pool. There were some stinging belly flops, but the pain was worth it when our *Fahnleinfuher,* the 15-year-old leader of our *Fahnlein* (literally "little flag"), a company-like unit of about 160 boys, handed us the coveted dagger with its inscription 'Blood and Honor.' From that moment on we were fully accepted."

—excerpt from Alfons Heck's *Diary of a Hitler Youth.*

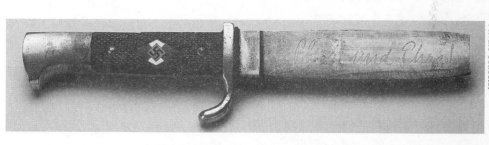

Both boys and girls wore a diamond-shaped pin like this on their Hitler Youth uniforms.

Boys wearing the "Blood and Honor" daggers of the Hitler Youth chanted slogans such as, "We are born to die for Germany."

Boys in the Hitler Youth participated in military training activities like camping and marksmanship, while girls focused on domestic chores and first aid. Both spent a lot of time on physical education. Boys had to be fit for combat and girls fit to bear numerous children.

Jungvolk Oath

Jungvolk had to take the following oath before a Nazi flag:

"In the presence of this blood banner, which represents our Fuehrer, I swear to devote all my energies and my strength to the savior of our country, Adolf Hitler. I am willing and ready to give up my life for him, so help me God."

HITS OF THE 1940S

Der Fuehrer's Face

When der Fuehrer says, "We ist der master race"
We HEIL! (phhht!) HEIL! (phhht!) Right in der Fuehrer's face
Not to love der Fuehrer is a great disgrace
So we HEIL! (phhht!) HEIL! (phhht!) Right in der Fuehrer's face
When Herr Goebbels says, "We own der world und space"
We HEIL! (phhht!) HEIL! (phhht!) Right in Herr Goebbels' face
When Herr Goering says they'll never bomb this place
We HEIL! (phhht!) HEIL! (phhht!) Right in Herr Goering's face

Are we not the supermen,
Aryan pure supermen?
Ja we ist der supermen,
Super-duper supermen!
Ist this Nutzi land not good?
Would you leave it if you could?
Ja this Nutzi land is good!
Vee would leave it if we could!

We bring the world to order,
Heil Hitler's new world order.
Everyone of foreign race will love der Fuehrer's face
When we bring to der world disorder.

When der Fuehrer says, "We ist der master race,"
We HEIL! (phhht!) HEIL! (phhht!) Right in der Fuehrer's face!
When der Fuehrer says, "We ist der master race,"
We HEIL! (phhht!) HEIL! (phhht!) Right in der Fuehrer's face!

Lili Marlene

Underneath the lantern by the barrack gate,
Darling I remember
the way you used to wait,
'Twas there that you whispered tenderly,
That you loved me,
You'd always be,
My Lili of the lamplight,
My own Lili Marlene.

Time would come for roll call,
Time for us to part,
Darling I'd caress you and
press you to my heart,
And there 'neath that far off lantern light,
I'd hold you tight,
We'd kiss "good-night,"
My Lili of the lamplight,
My own Lili Marlene.

Orders came for sailing
somewhere over there,
All confined to barracks
was more than I could bear;
I knew you were waiting in the street,
I heard your feet,
But could not meet,
My Lili of the lamplight,
My own Lili Marlene.

Resting in a billet
just behind the line,
Even though we're parted
your lips are close to mine;
You wait where that lantern softly gleams,
Your sweet face seems to haunt my dreams,
My Lili of the lamplight,
My own Lili Marlene.

Hulton/Getty Images

Marlene Dietrich with soldiers

Primary Sources Teaching Kit: World War II • Scholastic Teaching Resources

PROPAGANDA

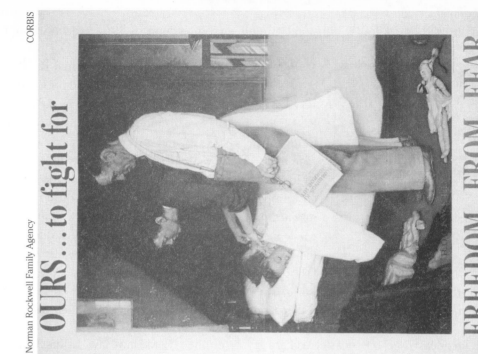

U.S. Poster : "Freedom From Fear"
Newspaper headline reads "BOMBING K . . . . HORROR HITS . . ."

Russian Poster: "Hit the Nazi Bug!"

Nazi Poster: "Youth in Aerial Defense!"

RADIO DAYS

As France's army collapsed, British Prime Minister Winston Churchill ended his June 18, 1940, speech with this passage:

". . . the Battle of France is over. I expect that the Battle of Britain is about to begin. Upon this battle depends the survival of Christian civilization. Upon it depends our own British life, and the long continuity of our institutions and our Empire. The whole fury and might of the enemy must very soon be turned on us. Hitler knows that he will have to break us in this Island or lose the war. If we can stand up to him, all Europe may be free and the life of the world may move forward into broad, sunlit uplands. But if we fail, then the whole world, including the United States, including all that we have known and cared for, will sink into the abyss of a new Dark Age made more sinister, and perhaps more protracted, by the lights of perverted science. Let us therefore brace ourselves to our duties, and so bear ourselves that, if the British Empire and its Commonwealth last for a thousand years, men will say, 'This was their finest hour.'"

In this August 2, 1940, radio broadcast, Nazi broadcaster William Joyce (dubbed "Lord Haw-Haw" by his British listeners) recounts Britain's many military disasters up till that time.

"No doubt the [British] soldiers fled [at Dunkirk] according to orders; no doubt they found themselves utterly at a loss to cope with the German dive-bombers and other engines of modern scientific warfare. . . . [This] brings us to the present time when German forces are destroying Britain's armament works, crippling her railways, closing her harbors, smashing her convoys, and sinking hundreds of thousands of tons each week of her tonnage, and when invasion is expected to come to her soil at any moment. . . . Well, it is clear that, when it comes to her own defense, England will be as weak as she was in defending her Allies. . . . However, what has been done is but a pale shadow of what is to come. The people of England will curse themselves for having preferred ruin from Churchill to peace from Hitler."

CBS radio correspondent Edward R. Murrow made this broadcast from London on September 13, 1940.

"This is London at three-thirty in the morning. This has been what might be called a 'routine night'—air-raid alarm at about nine o'clock and intermittent bombing ever since. . . . One becomes accustomed to rattling windows and the distant sound of bombs and then there comes a silence that can be felt. You know the sound will return—you wait, and then it starts again. That waiting is bad. It gives you a chance to imagine things. . . . Today I went to buy a hat—my favorite shop had gone, blown to bits. The windows of my shoe store were blown out. I decided to have a haircut; the windows of the barbershop were gone, but the Italian barber was still doing business. Someday, he said, we smile again, but the food it doesn't taste so good since being bombed. I went on to another shop to buy flashlight batteries. I bought three. The clerk said: 'You needn't buy so many. We'll have enough for the whole winter.' But I said: 'What if you aren't here?' There were buildings down in that street, and he replied: 'Of course we'll be here. We've been in business here for a hundred and fifty years.'"

MOVIES AT WAR

These two photographs show *Triumph of the Will* director Leni Riefenstahl. At right, she's seen filming high above the 1934 Nazi Nuremberg rally. The photograph below shows her (in light-colored dress) getting close-up shots of Nazi banners and soldiers.

In the 1942 American-made movie *Casablanca*, Nazi Major Strasser (holding the cigarette) is the movie's chief villain.

AIR WAR

The crew of Waddy's Wagon, posed according to the nose art portrait behind them, which reflects their jobs on board.

900 DAYS IN LENINGRAD

September 8, 1941–January 27, 1944

Russian poet Vera Inber wrote this passage in her diary on February 8, 1942, about five months after the siege began.

"In my mind's eye I constantly see a mother and daughter. . . . The mother—an old-age pensioner; her daughter Lyulya, sixteen years old, who is living with her. . . . Some dishonest woman tracked them down in a [food line], got to know them, wormed her way into their confidence, began to call on them at home, and finally promised to get Lyulya a job as a dish-washer at the 21st Military Hospital. . . . At the beginning of the month, when new ration cards were issued, this Lady Bountiful arrived to fetch the mother and daughter. She took both ration cards from the girl, her own and her mother's, for the entire month, also forty-five rubles in cash which the mother had borrowed. All this was allegedly to buy food . . . and instead she vanished into the darkness. . . . It is impossible to forget the mother and her daughter. The mother repeated in a heart-rending voice, again and again, 'Lyulya, what have you done to me! You have put me alive into my grave!' "

Eleven-year-old Tanya Savicheva kept a kind of diary of her relatives who died during the siege. She wrote the name of each one in an ABC notebook, putting it after the appropriate letter. (The dates are written in European style.)

Sovfoto/Eastfoto

Z – Zhenya died 28 December, 12:30 in the morning, 1941
B – Babushka died 25 January, 3 o'clock, 1942
L – Leka died 17 March, 5 o'clock in the morning, 1942
D – Dedya Vasya died 13 April, 2 o'clock at night, 1942
D – Dedya Lesha, 10 May, 4 o'clock in the afternoon, 1942
M – Mama, 13 May 7:30 a.m., 1942
S – Savichevs died. All died. Only Tanya remains.

900 DAYS IN LENINGRAD

Poster reads: "Death to child murderers!"

THE GATES OF AUSCHWITZ

Photo by SS-Unterscharfshrer Bernhart Walter, documenting the arrival, selection, and processing of Jews from Hungary, May 1944. The photo was taken for the "Auschwitz Album," a collection of photographs presented to the camp commandant.

Yad Vashem Archives/USHMM

Shortly after the war ended, SS corporal Pery Broad was captured by the British. He wrote this account of how the sorting process worked at Auschwitz.

"First the men and the women are divided. Heartbreaking scenes of farewell. Husbands and wives are separated, mothers wave to their sons for the last time.

"The lines of prisoners stand on the platform in ranks of five, several meters apart. If someone gives in to the pain of separation and runs to the other line again, to give his hand to one he loves, to whisper a few consoling words, a sharp blow from an SS man sends him staggering back.

"Now the SS doctor begins to segregate those who are fit for work, in his opinion, from those who are not. As a rule, mothers with little children are classed as not fit to work, as are those who look weak or sick. Wooden steps are brought to the back of the truck, and the ones the doctor selected as unfit for work have to get in. The SS men from the receiving unit count off everyone climbing the steps. Likewise they count all the ones fit for work, who have to start marching to the men's or women's camp. All the baggage must remain on the platform. The captives are told it will be taken later by truck. That is true, too, but none of the prisoners will ever see their property again."

THE GATES OF AUSCHWITZ

On May 31, 1944, thirteen-year-old Elli L. Friedmann arrived as a prisoner at Auschwitz. This was her experience with the sorting process.

Sometime during the fourth night, the train comes to a halt. We are awakened by the awful clatter of sliding doors being thrown open and cold air rushing into the wagon.

"'Raus! Alles 'raus!" (Get out! Get out!)

Rough voices. A figure clad in a striped uniform. Standing in the open doorway, illuminated from behind by an eerie diffused light, the figure looks like a creature from another planet.

"Schnell! 'Raus! Alles 'raus!" (Hurry! Get out!)

Two or three other such figures leap into the wagon and begin shoving the drowsy men, women, and children out into the cold night. A huge sign catches my eye: AUSCHWITZ.

The pain in my stomach sends a violent wave of nausea up my gullet.

The night is chilly and damp. An otherworldly glow lights up tall watchtowers, high wire fences, an endless row of cattle cars, SS men, dogs, and a mass of people pouring out of the wagons.

"'Raus! Los! 'Raus! 'Raus!"

Metal buttons glisten on SS uniforms.

"My things! I left everything in the wagon!"

"On line! Everyone stand on line! By fives! Men over there! Women and children over here!"

Mommy and Aunt Serena and I make only three. Two more women are shoved alongside us to make it five. Bubi [Elli's brother] is shoved farther, on the other side of the tracks. He turns to shout goodbye and trips on the wire fence flanking the tracks. Daddy's new gray hat rolls off his head. He reaches to pick it up. An SS man kicks him in the back, sending him tumbling onto the tracks.

Mother gasps. Aunt Serena gives a shriek and grasps Mommy's arm. I hold my mouth: A spasm of nausea hurls a charge of vomit up my throat.

"Marschieren! Los!" (March! Get going!)

The column of women, infants, and children begins to move. Dogs snarl, SS men scream orders, children cry, women weep good-byes to departing men, and I struggle with my convulsive stomach. And I march on. Next to me Mommy silently supports Aunt Serena by the shoulder. I march and the sounds and sights of Auschwitz only dimly penetrate my consciousness. Daylight is skirting the clouds and it turns very, very cold. We have left our coats in the wagon. We were ordered to leave all belongings in the wagon. Everything. We would get them later, we were told. How would they find what belongs to whom? There was such wild confusion at the train. Perhaps somehow they would sort things out. The Germans must have a system. They were famous for their order.

The marching column comes to a sudden halt. An officer in a gray SS uniform stands facing the lines. Dogs strain on leashes held by SS men flanking him on both sides. He stops each line and regroups them, sending some to his right and some to his left. Then he orders each group to march on. Fast.

I tremble as I stand before him. He looks at me with friendly eyes.

"Goldene Haar!" he exclaims and takes one of my long braids into his hands. I am not certain I heard right. Did he say "golden hair" about my braids?"

"Bist du Jüdin?" Are you Jewish?

The question startles me. "Yes, I am Jewish."

"Wie alt bist du?" How old are you.

"I am thirteen."

"You are tall for your age. Is this your mother? He touches Mommy lightly on the shoulder. "You go with your mother." With his riding stick he parts Aunt Serena from Mommy's embrace and gently shoves Mommy and me to the group moving to the right.

"Go. And remember, from now on you're sixteen."

Aunt Serena's eyes fill with terror. She runs to Mommy and grabs her arm.

"Don't leave me, Laura. Don't leave me!"

Mother hugs her fragile older sister and turns to the SS officer, her voice in a shrieking plea, "This is my sister, *Herr Offizier*, let me go with her! She is not feeling well. She needs me."

"You go with your daughter. She needs you more. March on! *Los!*" With an impatient move of his right hand he shoves Mother toward me. Then he glares angrily at Aunt Serena.

"Move on! *Los!* You go that way!"

His stick points menacingly to the left.

Aunt Serena, a forlorn, slight figure against the marching multitude, the huge German shepherd dogs, the husky SS men. A savage certainty slashes my bruised insides. I give an insane shriek, "Aunt Serena! Aunt Serena! I will never see you again!"

Wild fear floods her hazel eyes. She stretches out her arms to reach me. An SS soldier gives her a brutal thrust, hurling her into the line marching to the left. She turns again, mute dread lending her added fragility. She moves on.

I never saw Aunt Serena again.

DAY OF INFAMY

DRAFT No. 1   December 7, 1941.

PROPOSED MESSAGE TO THE CONGRESS

Yesterday, December 7, 1941, a date which will live in ~~world history~~ *infamy* → *of Japanese*

the United States of America was ~~simultaneously~~ *suddenly* and deliberately attacked

by naval and air forces of the Empire of Japan.

The United States was at the moment at peace with that nation and was ~~continuing the~~ *still in* conversations with its Government and its Emperor looking

toward the maintenance of peace in the Pacific. Indeed, one hour after

Japanese air squadrons had commenced bombing in ~~Hawaii and the Philippines~~ *Oahu*

the Japanese Ambassador to the United States and his colleague delivered

to the Secretary of State a formal reply to a ~~former~~ *recent American* message. ~~from the Secretary.~~ *While* This reply ~~contained a statement~~ *stated* that diplomatic negotiations *it seemed useless to continue* ~~must be considered at an end, but~~ *it* contained no threat ~~and no~~ hint of *or* war or

armed attack.

It will be recorded that the distance ~~of Manila, but especially~~ of

Hawaii from Japan makes it obvious that the *y* attack ~~were~~ *was* deliberately

or some weeks planned many days ago. During the intervening time the Japanese Govern-

ment has deliberately sought to deceive the United States by false

statements and expressions of hope for continued peace.

DRAFT NO. 1   -2-

The attack yesterday on ~~Hawaii and on the Island of Oahu~~ *the Hawaiian Islands* has

caused severe damage to American naval and military forces. Very

many American lives have been lost. In addition American ~~ships~~ ships

have been torpedoed on the high seas between San Francisco and

Honolulu.

Yesterday the Japanese Government also launched an attack

against Malaya. *Last night Japanese forces attacked Guam.* Japan has, therefore, undertaken a surprise offensive *extending the Philippine Islands*

throughout the Pacific area. The facts of yesterday speak for

themselves. The people of the United States have already formed

their opinions and well understand the implications ~~to the very~~

~~life and~~ safety of our nation.

As Commander-in-Chief of the Army and Navy I have ~~directed~~,

directed that all measures be taken for our defense.

Long will we remember the character of the onslaught against

us.

(A) *No matter how long it may take us to overcome this premeditated invasion the American people will in their righteous might win through to absolute victory.*

DRAFT NO. 1   -3-

I speak the will of the Congress and of the people ~~of this~~

~~country~~ when I assert that we will not only defend ourselves to

the uttermost but will see to it that this form of treachery shall

never endanger us again. Hostilities exist. There is no mincing

the fact that our people, our territory and our interests are in

grave danger.

I, therefore, ask that the Congress declare that since the

unprovoked and dastardly attack by Japan on Sunday, December

seventh, a state of war exists *has* between the United States and the

Japanese Empire.

----

with confidence in their might

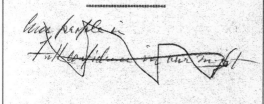

DAY OF INFAMY

This is the text of the war message that President Franklin D. Roosevelt delivered to Congress on December 8, 1941. (Original with edits by FDR shown on page 31.)

Mr. Vice-President, Mr. Speaker, members of the Senate and of the House of Representatives:

Yesterday, December 7, 1941—a date which will live in infamy—the United States of America was suddenly and deliberately attacked by naval and air forces of the Empire of Japan.

The United States was at peace with that nation, and at the solicitation of Japan, was still in conversation with its government and its Emperor looking toward the maintenance of peace in the Pacific.

Indeed, one hour after Japanese air squadrons had commenced bombing in the American island of Oahu, the Japanese Ambassador to the United States and his colleague delivered to our Secretary of State a formal reply to a recent American message. While this reply stated that it seemed useless to continue the existing diplomatic negotiations, it contained no threat or hint of war or armed attack.

It will be recorded that the distance of Hawaii from Japan makes it obvious that the attack was deliberately planned many days or even weeks ago. During the intervening time the Japanese government has deliberately sought to deceive the United States by false statements and expressions of hope for continued peace.

The attack yesterday on the Hawaiian Islands has caused severe damage to American naval and military forces. I regret to tell you that many American lives have been lost. In addition, American ships have been reported torpedoed on the high seas between San Francisco and Honolulu.

Yesterday the Japanese government also launched an attack against Malaya.

Last night Japanese forces attacked Hongkong.

Last night Japanese forces attacked Guam.

Last night Japanese forces attacked the Philippine Islands.

Last night the Japanese attacked Wake Island.

And this morning the Japanese attacked Midway Island.

Japan has, therefore, undertaken a surprise offensive extending throughout the Pacific area. The facts of yesterday and today speak for themselves. The people of the United States have already formed their opinions and well understand the implications to the very life and safety of our nation.

As Commander in Chief of the Army and Navy I have directed that all measures be taken for our defense.

Always will our whole nation remember the character of the onslaught against us.

No matter how long it may take us to overcome this premeditated invasion, the American people in their righteous might will win through to absolute victory.

I believe I interpret the will of the Congress and of the people when I assert that we will not only defend ourselves to the uttermost but will make it very certain that this form of treachery shall never again endanger us.

Hostilities exist. There is no blinking at the fact that our people, our territories and our interests are in grave danger.

With confidence in our armed forces—with the unbounding determination of our people—we will gain the inevitable triumph—so help us God.

I ask that the Congress declare that since the unprovoked and dastardly attack by Japan on Sunday, Dec. 7, 1941, a state of war has existed between the United States and the Japanese Empire.

Pearl Harbor under attack, December 7, 1941.

SOLDIER LIFE

estate of Bill Mauldin

"Fresh, spirited American troops, flushed with victory, are bringing in thousands of hungry, ragged, battle-weary prisoners . . . "

"Them buttons wuz shot off when I took this town, sir."

Dig a hole in your back yard while it is raining. Sit in the hole until the water climbs up around your ankles. Pour cold mud down your shirt collar. Sit there for forty-eight hours, and, so there is no danger of your dozing off, imagine that a guy is sneaking around waiting for a chance to club you on the head or set your house on fire.

Get out of the hole, fill a suitcase full of rocks, pick it up, put a shotgun in your other hand, and walk on the muddiest road you can find. Fall flat on your face every few minutes as you imagine big meteors streaking down to sock you.

After ten or twelve miles (remember—you are still carrying the shotgun and suitcase) start sneaking through the wet brush. Imagine that somebody has booby-trapped your route with rattlesnakes which will bite you if you step on them. Give some friend a rifle and have them blast in your direction once in a while.

Snoop around until you find a bull. Try to figure out a way to sneak around him without letting him see you. When he does see you, run . . . all the way back to your hole in the backyard, drop the suitcase and shotgun, and get in.

If you repeat this performance every three days for several months you may begin to understand why an infantryman sometimes gets out of breath. But you still won't understand how he feels when things get tough.

— from *Up Front, 1943–44*
by soldier-cartoonist Bill Mauldin

SOLDIER LIFE

Marine Lt. William Ellison was a dive-bomber pilot who fought in a major battle off Guadalcanal on November 30, 1942. Ellison won the Distinguished Flying Cross for his actions, which included eluding Japanese fighters, going through heavy antiaircraft fire, and then finding his way home safely after getting lost in fog. On December 31, Ellison wrote about his experiences in that battle to a friend in Amenia, New York. He concluded his letter this way:

You can live and do this and still think about other things. You can get scared to death in the morning, come through it, and spend the afternoon reading or playing cards. There is nothing great about it. It is what you have been trained for and have become used to, and in a way it is routine. This is not trying to be smart but to explain it.

Before I came out here I always thought that so-called "physical courage" was one overrated virtue and it sure is. You can have it if you want it. The guys who have proved yellow were mentally yellow in the first place. And for my money the guys who think this is all, the greatest, and the highest mode of living are also full of bull, because it isn't and there is plenty more.

We have been here for over five weeks, and the things that at first seemed strange are now becoming routine. It is impressive how adaptable people are, how they make the best of things without consciously thinking they are doing so. This is amazing and wonderful to me, especially as the assorted smallnesses seem to go on, petty jealousies, irritability, ego blossoms and so on.

And one thing I don't mean to say, by golly, is that war brings out beautiful attributes in people, because it doesn't. But it does show an energy and natural worth that should give a lot of promise if it were later put to better more building-up use.

I think I can put up an argument against the group that accuses our generation of being incurably desiccated, degenerate, nihilistic, unenthusiastic, et al. There is enthusiasm and vigor in these guys that cannot be pooh-poohed even by the most agile tearer-downers nor cheapened by the most blatant builder-uppers.

HOME FRONT I

National Archives

HOME FRONT I

Museum of World War II

COPY.

WESTERN UNION

NEWCOMB CARLTON
CHAIRMAN OF THE BOARD

N. B. WHITE
PRESIDENT

J. C. WILLEVER
FIRST VICE-PRESIDENT

CLASS OF SERVICE DESIRED		
DOMESTIC		CABLE
TELEGRAM		FULL RATE
DAY LETTER		DEFERRED
NIGHT MESSAGE		NIGHT LETTER
NIGHT LETTER		SHIP RADIOGRAM

Patrons should check class of service desired; otherwise message will be transmitted as a full-rate communication.

Send the following message, subject to the terms on back hereof, which are hereby agreed to

P.WA.360 IB7C5W 77 Gov't. = extra Check U.S. Delivery OR 01 C=
TX Washington D.C. 20 1[?] 1[?] F 141 Dec. 21 A.M. 12 19

Martin John Scheuerlein--
3745 N. Percy Street-Philadelphia Pa.

The Navy Department deeply regrets to notify you that your
son, George Albert Scheuerlein, Gunners mate third class, U.S.
N, is missing following action in the performance of his duty
and in the service of his country X The government appreciates
your great anxiety and will furnish you further information
promptly when received X To prevent possible aid to our enemy
please do not divulge the name of his ship or station--

Rear Admiral Randall Jacobs Chief of the Bureau of Navigation

THE QUICKEST, SUREST AND SAFEST WAY TO SEND MONEY IS BY TELEGRAPH OR CABLE

Project 2 — Page 214

HOME FRONT II

Internee Miné Okubo published *Citizen 13660* in 1946 after her release from Topaz Relocation Center, an internment camp for Japanese Americans in Utah. Here are four pages from the book.

It was no use just sitting there, so we went to work cleaning the stall. We took turns sweeping the floor with a whisk broom. It was the only practical thing we had brought with us.

There was a lack of privacy everywhere. The incomplete partitions in the stalls and the barracks made a single symphony of yours and your neighbors' loves, hates, and joys. One had to get used to snores, baby-crying, family troubles, and even to the jitterbugs.

The center had a canteen, but on most days there was nothing to buy.

"Line-ups here and line-ups there" describes our daily life. We lined up for mail, for checks, for meals, for showers, for washrooms, for laundry tubs, for toilets, for clinic service, for movies. We lined up for everything.

Columbia University Press

WOMEN AT WAR

Minneapolis Journal

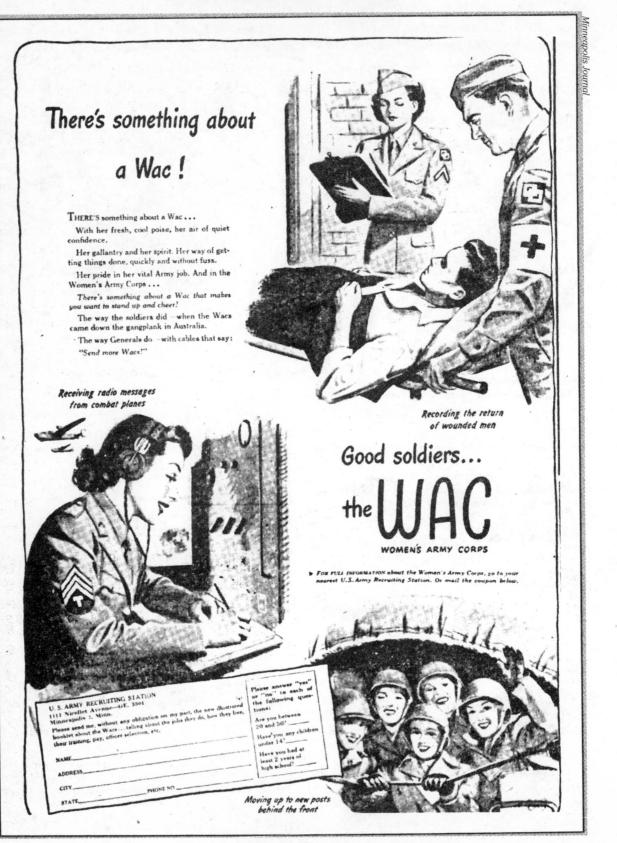

There's something about a Wac!

THERE'S something about a Wac . . .

With her fresh, cool poise, her air of quiet confidence.

Her gallantry and her spirit. Her way of getting things done, quickly and without fuss.

Her pride in her vital Army job. And in the Women's Army Corps . . .

There's something about a Wac that makes you want to stand up and cheer!

The way the soldiers did — when the Wacs came down the gangplank in Australia.

The way Generals do — with cables that say: "Send more Wacs!"

Receiving radio messages from combat planes

Recording the return of wounded men

Good soldiers...
the WAC
WOMEN'S ARMY CORPS

▶ FOR FULL INFORMATION about the Women's Army Corps, go to your nearest U.S. Army Recruiting Station. Or mail the coupon below.

U.S. ARMY RECRUITING STATION
1111 Nicollet Avenue—4-E, 3501
Minneapolis 3, Minn.

Please send me, without any obligation on my part, the new illustrated booklet about the Wacs . . . telling about the jobs they do, how they live, their training, pay, officer selection, etc.

NAME_____

ADDRESS_____

CITY_____

STATE_____ PHONE NO.____

Please answer "yes" or "no" to each of the following questions!

Are you between 20 and 50?_____

Have you any children under 14?____

Have you had at least 2 years of high school?_____

Moving up to new posts behind the front

Newspaper recruitment ad for the Women's Army Corps.

WOMEN AT WAR

1940s U.S. government poster advertising jobs
in military industry for women.

"Beltline Girl" 1942

I stood on the station platform
And looked at the lonesome track.
The train had gone around the curve
The train that might never come back
For it carried my soldier sweetheart away
The one I loved so true.
My heart was sad, but I did not weep
I thought of the work to do.

*J*oe had gone to the fighting front
And he left his job behind
Now I must step into his place
On the long assembly line.
I said I'll learn to build a ship
I'll learn to build a plane
For the faster we speed this belt line, girls,
The quicker our boys return.

*I*f you think that danger is far away
And cannot reach our shore
Go ask the wives of MacArthur's men,
They'll tell you about this war.
Go ask the widows of the Pearl Harbor boys
Our heroines brave and fine
You'll find them at work in the training schools
And on the assembly line.

*I*f a thousand men leave a thousand jobs
to go and fight the foe,
Our factory wheels would slacken their speed
And the belts would move too slow.
But when a thousand hard-working girls
Step in and take a hand
Out roll the tanks and planes and guns
And there's freedom in the land.

A FIGHT TO THE DEATH

This is from the Japanese military's First Order to the Kamikazes.

> ". . . It is absolutely out of the question for you to return alive. Your mission involves certain death. . . . The death of a single one of you will be the birth of a million others. Neglect nothing that may affect your training or your health. . . . And, lastly, do not be in too much of a hurry to die. If you cannot find your target, turn back; next time you may find a more favorable opportunity. Choose a death which brings about a maximum result."

Kamikaze pilot Akio Otsuka wrote a letter to his family during the two days before his death. Here is an excerpt.

"Do not weep because I am about to die. If I were to live and one of my dear ones to die, I would do all in my power to cheer those who remain behind. I would try to be brave.

"11:30 a.m.—the last morning. I shall now have breakfast and then go to the aerodrome. I am busy with my final briefing and have not time to write any more. So I bid you farewell.

"Excuse this illegible letter and the jerky sentences.

"Keep in good health.

"I believe in the victory of Greater Asia.

"I pray for the happiness of you all, and I beg your forgiveness for my lack of piety.

"I leave for the attack with a smile on my face. The moon will be full to-night. As I fly over the open sea off Okinawa I will choose the enemy ship that is to be my target.

"I will show you that I know how to die bravely.

"With all my respectful affection.

"Akio Otsuka"

A kamikaze suicide plane dives toward a U.S. warship in October 1944.

HIROSHIMA

AP/Wide World Photos

This building, the Hiroshima Prefecture Industrial Promotion Hall, was the only one left standing near the bomb's blast. Today, its ruins are preserved as the Hiroshima Peace Memorial.

John Van Hasselt/CORBIS Sygma

This stopped watch found in the rubble records the time of the explosion.

National Archives

Hiroshima Peace Memorial Museum

The intense heat caused by the blast fused these glass bottles together.

The first sign of the bomb was a blinding white light. It etched the shadows of objects and people onto walls and sidewalks instantaneously.

AFTERMATH

Statistics

WORLD WAR I (1914–1918)

Nations involved: 28

Estimated military death toll: 8 million to 10 million plus

Estimated civilian death toll: 7 million to 14 million plus

American military death toll: 116,516 (53,402 combat; 63,114 disease, other causes)

Estimated total cost: $337 billion (1918 dollars)

Estimated American cost: $26 billion

WORLD WAR II (1939–1945)

Nations involved: 59

Estimated military death toll: 14 million to 50 million plus

Estimated civilian death toll: 17 million to 50 million plus

American military death toll: 405,399 (291,557 combat; 113,842 disease, other causes)

Estimated total cost: More than $1 trillion (1945 dollars)

Estimated American cost: $288 billion

American servicemen and -women gather in Paris to celebrate the unconditional surrender of the Japanese, August 15, 1945.

Army News Features

AFTERMATH

Quotes

Life under tyranny

"The funny thing was that in Germany life went on as normal in some ways, people fell in love, dinner was cooked, children cared for, yet sudden jolts, like the invasion of France and the talk of the SS at dinner, brought home the truth of the iniquitous core—one man's desire to dominate, to have power over his fellow men."

—*Christabel Bielenberg, an Englishwoman married to a German*

Life as a soldier

"When we landed on Omaha Beach [on D-Day] some of the biggest guys, and high-ranking officers, lay down and broke into uncontrollable crying and kicking their feet and screaming, "I want mama," but most of us kept going. We kept going because we were somewhat insane from what we were facing. Looking back I realize the hysterics were the only sane ones. They were the only ones who knew what was happening."

—*Charles Feinstein, U.S. Army*

Germany's surrender

"There won't be any more dying, any more raids. It's over. But the fear set in of what would happen afterwards. We were spiritually and emotionally drained. Hitler's doctrines were discredited. . . . Surviving, finding something to eat and drink, was less difficult for me than the psychological emptiness. It was incomprehensible that all this was supposed to be over, and that it had all been for nothing."

—*Anna Hummel, a dedicated German Nazi who survived the war*

Japan's surrender

"The Emperor spoke in Court Japanese and only Terry could comprehend. As Terry translated and [Japanese civilians] grasped the sense of what as being said, that it meant surrender, the bandaged woman began to weep —not loudly or hysterically but with deep sobs that racked her body. The children started crying and before the Emperor had finished, all his people were weeping audibly."

—*Gwen Terasaki, an American married to a Japanese official*

The Holocaust

From "On a Sunny Evening"

The sun has made a veil of gold
So lovely that my body aches.
Above, the heavens shriek with blue
Convinced I've smiled by some mistake.
The world's abloom and seems to smile.
I want to fly but where, how high?
If in barbed wire, things can bloom
Why couldn't I? I will not die!

—*Anonymous, 1944; written by children in Barracks L318 and L417 at Terezin concentration camp*

The smell of death

"There's only one stink and that's it. You never get used to it, either. As long as you live, you never get used to it. And after a while, the stink gets in your clothes and you can taste it in your mouth. You know what I think? I think maybe if every civilian in the world could smell this stink, then maybe we wouldn't have any more wars."

—*Donald Haguall, U.S. Army, assigned to a unit that buried the war dead*

The postwar world

"I am sure that in the past two years I have heard soldiers say a thousand times 'If only we could have created all this energy for something good.' . . . All we can do is fumble and try once more—try out of the memory of our anguish— and be as tolerant with each other as we can."

—*Ernie Pyle, U.S. war correspondent*

WORLD WAR II
K-W-L CHART

In the K-W-L chart below, write down what you already know about World War II in the *K* box, and then write what you want to learn in the *W* box.

What I KNOW

What I WANT to Know

What I LEARNED

When you've found the answers to your questions, record your discoveries in the What I Learned box *(L)*, and new questions in the What I Still Want to Learn box.

What I Still Want to Learn

Name _____ Date _____

WORLD WAR II MAP

Show what you know about the events, alliances, and territorial divisions of World War II.

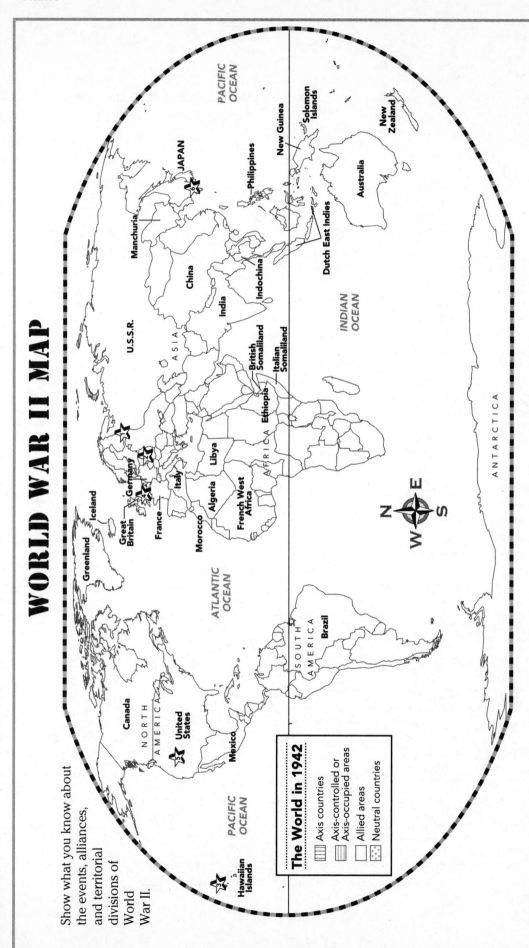

The World in 1942

- ▦ Axis countries
- ▥ Axis-controlled or Axis-occupied areas
- ☐ Allied areas
- ⦂ Neutral countries

A. Identify the three Axis countries with vertical lines. (See "Axis countries" in the key.)

B. Mark the territory they conquered at the height of their power in 1942 with horizontal lines. (See "Axis-controlled or Axis-occupied areas" in the key.)

C. Show all Allied-controlled areas with a dark outline. (See "Allied areas" in the key.)

D. Highlight neutral countries with a pattern of dots. (See "Neutral countries" in the key.)

E. Use the following clues to identify the six stars on this map. All are important wartime locations.

1. City besieged by Nazi Germany for about 900 days: _____

2. Largest Nazi extermination camp, located in Poland: _____

3. Site of a surprise attack by the Japanese : _____

4. City bombed heavily during the Battle of Britain: _____

5. Place in Utah where Japanese Americans were sent: _____

6. The two cities bombed using atomic weapons: _____

45

World War II Glossary

Use this glossary to understand the meaning of some words and phrases from World War II. Add other terms to this glossary as you study the war. You may want to incorporate some of these terms as you write your stories, using the ideas below.

Allies
coalition of countries led by Great Britain, the United States, and the Soviet Union that fought against the Axis

appeasement
to give something to a bully in hopes of stopping further aggression

Axis
coalition of countries led by Germany, Italy, and Japan that fought against the Allies

GI
short for "government issue"; became most popular nickname for U.S. soldiers

Holocaust
Hitler's "Final Solution" or extermination of Jews. The Holocaust resulted in the deaths of at least six million Jews and five million other victims of Nazi camps and firing squads, including political prisoners, Jehovah's Witnesses, and others deemed dangerous to the survival of Germany.

kamikaze
Japanese for "divine wind," it became the name of suicide pilots who attacked Allied ships

Nazi
abbreviation for the National Socialist German Workers' Party

propaganda
a one-sided communication designed to shape opinions

rationing
limits imposed on buying certain products and services to preserve resources (began in 1942 in the United States)

Rosie the Riveter
nickname given to U.S. women who entered the job force in World War II (from a Norman Rockwell character painted in 1943)

SS
Abbreviation for *Shutzstaffel*, an elite Nazi military and police force

Story Starter Tips!

If you choose to write a narrative account about World War II, here are some suggestions to get you started:

Dear Hans, We have been close friends for many years. But now that the Nazis have come to power, you refuse to speak to me because I am Jewish. . . .

My sister began running through the house yelling "They've bombed Pearl Harbor! They've bombed Pearl Harbor!" "Who was 'they,' " I asked myself, "and where is Pearl Harbor?". . .

It was a beautiful fall day. Bright autumn reds, oranges, and yellows mixed with green pine trees as they swayed in the cool breeze. Nothing could have been more perfect. Then a car pulled up outside our house. I could see it was the Western Union man. . . .

The Japanese plane was bearing down on our ship, and none of our guns seemed to stop it. The plane began a crazy spiral that sent it headed straight for my battle station. The other guys and I had to think fast. . . .

WORLD WAR II JOURNAL

WORLD WAR II MAP ANSWER KEY

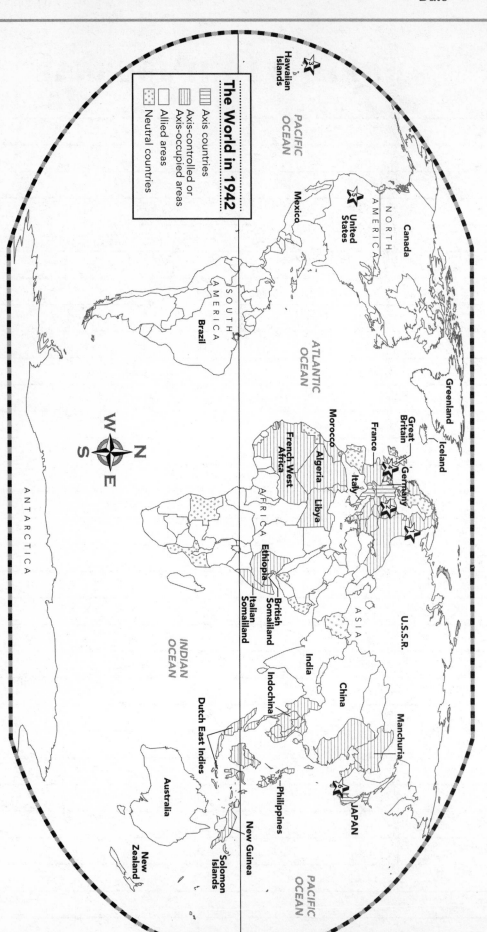

The World in 1942

- ▨ Axis countries
- ▥ Axis-controlled or Axis-occupied areas
- ⬚ Allied areas
- ☐ Neutral countries

Map labels:
PACIFIC OCEAN
Hawaiian Islands
Mexico
Canada
NORTH AMERICA
United States
SOUTH AMERICA
Brazil
ATLANTIC OCEAN
Greenland
Iceland
Great Britain
France
Germany
Morocco
Algeria
French West Africa
Italy
Libya
Ethiopia
British Somaliland
Italian Somaliland
AFRICA
ANTARCTICA
INDIAN OCEAN
U.S.S.R.
India
China
Indochina
Manchuria
ASIA
Dutch East Indies
Philippines
New Guinea
JAPAN
Solomon Islands
Australia
New Zealand
PACIFIC OCEAN

1. Leningrad, Soviet Union
2. Auschwitz
3. Pearl Harbor, Hawaii
4. London
5. Topaz Relocation Center
6. Hiroshima and Nagasaki, Japan